392-   11982

3

DATE DUE		
OCT 9 '82		
FEB 28		
JUN 2		
JUL 11		
APR 1 1991		
JAN 13 1991		
APR 07 2005		
JUL 08 2010		

INDIANS OF AMERICA

Chief Joseph
OF THE NEZ PERCE

MATTHEW G. GRANT

Illustrated by John Keely

11982

GALLERY OF GREAT AMERICANS SERIES

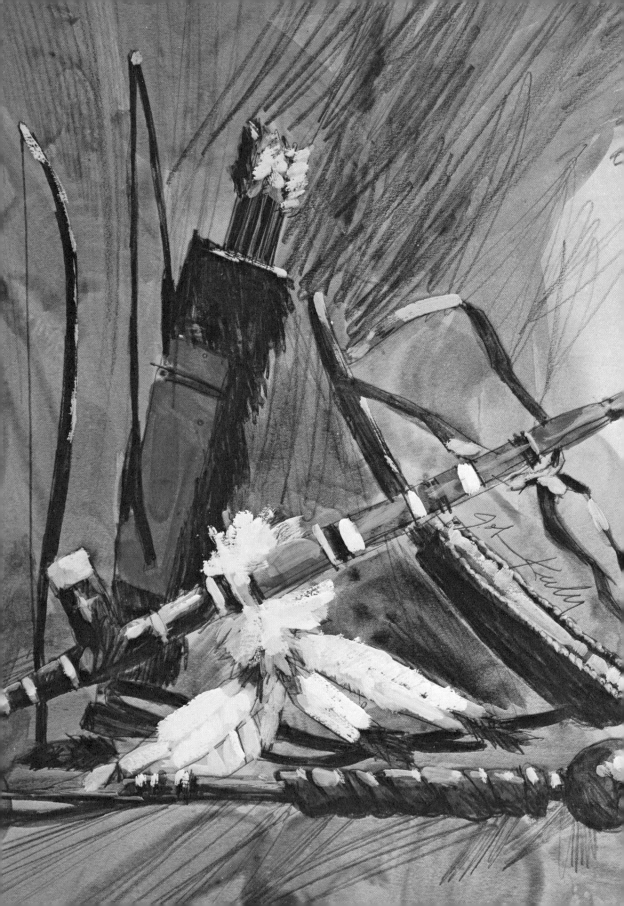

Chief Joseph
OF THE NEZ PERCE

Text copyright © 1974 by Publications Associates. Illustrations copyright © 1974 by Creative Education. International copyrights reserved in all countries. No part of this book may be reproduced in any form without written permission from the publisher. Printed in the United States.

Library of Congress Number: 73-9816

ISBN: O-87191-251-1

Published by Creative Education, Mankato, Minnesota 56001
Distributed by Childrens Press, 1224 West Van Buren Street,
Chicago, Illinois 60607

Library of Congress Cataloging in Publication Data
Grant, Matthew G
    Chief Joseph of the Nez Percé.
    At head of title: Indians of America.
    SUMMARY: Biography of the Nez Percé Chief who in a dispute with the United States Army successfully led his outnumbered tribe on a one-thousand mile retreat.
    1. Joseph, Nez Percé chief, 1840-1904—Juvenile literature. [1. Joseph, Nez Percé chief, 1840-1904. 2. Nez Percé Indians—Biography. 3. Indians of North America—Biography]
I. Keely, John, illus.   II. Title. E99.N5J583 970.3 [B] [92] 73-9816
ISBN 0-87191-251-1

CONTENTS

THE NEZ PERCE TRIBE

Beyond the Rocky Mountains, in lands that are now part of Oregon, Idaho, and Washington, lived a strong Indian tribe. The people called themselves Nimpau. But white explorers who found them gave them the name Nez Perce Indians.

7

The tribe lived along the great rivers of that country. They caught salmon. The women dug roots and made good food from them. And from time to time the men went east over the mountains to hunt buffalo.

The Nez Perce people had beautiful spotted horses that we now call Appaloosas. The tribe was proud and well-to-do. When white men came into their country, the Indians treated them well. White men had power — and the Nez Perce admired it.

The chiefs wanted their people to be as clever and rich as the white traders. They

asked for white teachers, and so missionaries and their families went to the Nez Perce.

Many of the Indians became Christians. They thought that if they did this, they would gain some of the white man's power. One of the most important Christian chiefs was Old Joseph, who lived in the Wallowa Valley. About 1840, a son was born to the chief.

The missionaries called the boy "Young Joseph." When he was five or six years old, he went to the mission school.

In 1847, trouble came to the white missionaries. Deadly sickness infected the Cayuse tribe, neighbors to the Nez Perce. The Cayuse blamed the white people, and killed 12 of them. The U.S. Army was sent to punish the Cayuse.

Old Joseph watched the missionaries flee. He thought: "Perhaps the white religion is not so strong after all."

Several years went by. The chief and his family were no longer Christians. They had returned to the old religion of their people. They called the Earth their mother and loved the land. When he was ten years old, Young Joseph went off alone to pray to the Great Spirit, the Maker-of-All, just as all young men of his tribe did. As he prayed, he was given a vision. He heard a voice give him a name: Thunder-Rolling-in-the-Mountains. It was a name of great power.

BROKEN PROMISES

The chief's son grew older. He became
a hunter and a warrior. But more than this,
he was wise and honorable. He worried, as
his father did, when more and more white
people poured into the Indian lands. Trouble
lay ahead.

In 1855, the U.S. government made a treaty with the Nez Perce. The tribe promised to live only on a reservation in the Wallowa Valley. In return, the government would pay money, food, and supplies. Even though the government did not keep its promises, the Nez Perce kept theirs. They stayed at peace with the whites for more than 15 years.

But now gold miners and settlers invaded the reservation. And Old Joseph, the chief, was dying.

The old man called his son. He said:

"My son, now you will be the chief of these people. They look to you to guide them.

You must stop your ears if white men ask you to sign a treaty and sell your home. A few more years and the white men will be all around you. They have their eyes on this land. But never forget my dying words! This country holds your father's body. Never sell the bones of your father and your mother."

THE YOUNG CHIEF

In 1871, Thunder-Rolling-in-the-Mountains became chief of his people. The white leaders called him Chief Joseph, and this is the name that has gone down in history. From the first, he set out to fulfill the promise made to his father.

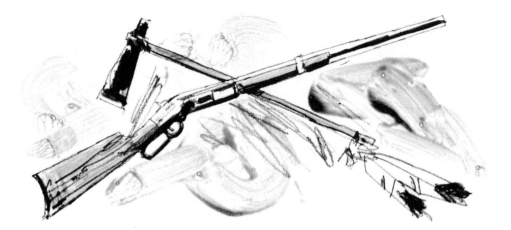

Many white ranchers came to live in the Wallowa Valley Reservation. The government tried to make a new treaty with the tribe. Chief Joseph's people were told to move north, to another reservation.

But they refused. The chief remembered the old promises that had been broken. Why should he believe new promises?

"You *must* move," the government agents said.

Joseph replied: ''This land is our mother. We will not go.''

Finally, in May of 1877, the U.S. Army was sent to the valley to force the Nez Perce onto the new reservation.

Chief Joseph saw that many warriors were ready to fight. He tried to prevent bloodshed by urging the people to pack up and leave. Sad and angry, they left their home forever.

Burdened by children, old people, cattle, ponies, and goods, they could only travel very slowly. They met Chief White Bird's band at Rocky Canyon and made camp.

Hot-headed young men called for white blood. Joseph could not stop them from riding out. The young warriors murdered four white men, then came back to say:

"Now you will have to fight with us. Soon the soldiers will be here. Prepare for war! Prepare for war!"

For years, Joseph had worked for peace. But now the people rose up in fury. All of the other chiefs wanted war. Joseph, their leader, could only follow.

23

Bands of warriors attacked white settlements. Army troops sent after the Nez Perce rode into an ambush at White Bird Canyon. The army forces were crushed by the red men. It was the worst white defeat since the Battle of the Little Big Horn the year before.

The happy Indians celebrated their victory. But Joseph knew that a black future lay ahead. More soldiers would be coming. What would happen to the people then?

Now Chief Joseph took cammand once more. He proved to be the military equal of General O. O. Howard, who was sent out to capture him. Howard had about 600 soldiers. Joseph had perhaps 200 warriors, with 400 more women, children, and old people. It should have been easy for the white army to subdue the refugee band.

But Chief Joseph seemed to outwit the white general at every turn. The Indians won fight after fight.

THE LONG RETREAT

Chief Joseph planned to lead his people to Canada, as Sitting Bull had done after the Battle of Little Big Horn. But the border was more than 1,000 miles away. Many people were sick or wounded. Nevertheless, they started northward.

Again and again the white army tried
to trap the Nez Perce. But the warriors fought
the troops and won, while the people escaped.
All over the United States, people read about
the war and marveled at the skill of the red
men, led by Chief Joseph. He took them over
high mountains, through trackless wilderness.
For four months they traveled, until winter was

upon them. Then, 30 miles from the Canadian border, Chief Joseph and his people were surrounded. It was the end.

Chief Joseph rode forward alone toward General Howard and General Nelson A. Miles. With dignity, he gave them his rifle. Then he said:

"Tell General Howard I know his heart. . . . I am tired of fighting. Our chiefs are killed. . . . It is cold and we have no blankets. The little children are freezing. We have no food. Hear me, my chiefs. I am tired. My heart is sick and sad. From where the sun now stands, I will fight no more forever."

White men had promised Chief Joseph that his people would be returned to their own country. But once again, the white promise was broken. The Nez Perce were sent to Kansas, then to the Indian Territory (now Oklahoma). Many died there.

Finally, in 1885, Joseph and his band went to a reservation in the state of Washington. The chief spent the rest of his life trying to make the government fulfill its promises. He died September 21, 1904, still waiting.

★ ★
GALLERY OF GREAT AMERICANS SERIES
★ ★

INDIANS OF AMERICA

GERONIMO
CRAZY HORSE
CHIEF JOSEPH
PONTIAC
SQUANTO
OSCEOLA

EXPLORERS OF AMERICA

COLUMBUS
LEIF ERICKSEN
DeSOTO
LEWIS AND CLARK
CHAMPLAIN
CORONADO

FRONTIERSMEN OF AMERICA

DANIEL BOONE
BUFFALO BILL
JIM BRIDGER
FRANCIS MARION
DAVY CROCKET
KIT CARSON

WAR HEROES OF AMERICA

JOHN PAUL JONES
PAUL REVERE
ROBERT E. LEE
ULYSSES S. GRANT
SAM HOUSTON
LAFAYETTE

WOMEN OF AMERICA

CLARA BARTON
JANE ADAMS
ELIZABETH BLACKWELL
HARRIET TUBMAN
SUSAN B. ANTHONY
DOLLY MADISON

★ ★